{MAKE IT HAPPEN!}

A "GET IT DONE" GUIDE FOR DREAMERS AND VISIONARIES

Kate Siner, Ph.D

www.katesiner.com

TABLE OF CONTENTS

Introduction

I have met and worked with several people who have had really good ideas. They aspire, in one way or another and in varying degrees, to make the world a better place. They sense a need - at first, from a very personal place, but with the potential to become so much more; they want to realize their aspirations.

Unfortunately, many people who have these types of visions do not have the skills they need to achieve them. Vision itself is not enough. As a result, these people might complain about not knowing where to get started, not being certain if their plan is viable, or not being clear about how to get others on board. These difficulties may leave them wondering if the world needs their vision or whether they are just another crazy dreamer.

ARE YOU ONE OF THESE PEOPLE?

I believe that the seed of the dream that you are carrying in your heart is also the dream of the world around you and the world is waiting for your work. But just because the world is waiting doesn't mean you will get an invitation to make your vision a reality. Others cannot always ask for what you have - because you are the one with the vision. One of the first obstacles to your success is your self-doubt. I believe full heartedly that you hold that seed but do you?

Even if you have a strong belief it is likely to be tested by some resistance. You might meet, and may already have met, some. This resistance can take the form of doubting thoughts inside and outside of you. While, in time, you might come to see even this inner resistance as an ally, it is essential that it does not stop you before you even start. If it does, you will lose something very important - the very light to which you are the guardian.

I wrote this brief guide as a means of helping people manifest their good, heart-centered ideas and visionary-type plans. In this guide, I offer some basic, but essential, tools to help you clarify your vision and move it more rapidly into reality.

The Visionary

Historically, a visionary has been defined as someone who has had a spiritual experience providing insights about the future - for the individual, his or her community, or the world at large. Joan of Arc is a well-known example.

Visionaries exist in all walks of life. For example, in the Utne Reader, (November-December 2009) 50 contemporary visionaries were named: poets, activists, inventors, CEOs, and more. Heading up the list was the Dalai Lama. But for the purposes of this guide - giving fledgling visionaries the necessary tools for flight - it is not so much what visionaries do as the way they do it.

For our purposes, we will be using a more generalized definition. I consider a visionary to be someone who sees something that does not exist - but which might benefit others - and brings it into reality.

The Call

Some of us have an inner voice that calls us down a different track from the well-worn ones laid down by our culture. We don't know why. Sometimes we don't even realize it - we are just different from our peers. Some of us are successful adapting to this difference; however, some of us have a hard time fitting in anywhere.

The common thread among these people is that their road is not the road most take. Sometimes we are even forced off the main drag due to life's circumstances, but we come to a deeper understanding of the role we are meant to play because of it. Sometimes there is a longing - maybe a barely-audible voice that calls us forward. Eventually, if we pay attention, we can determine what this "voice" is saying. However, if we find ways to block the voice out, we grow unhappy and wither. We just know that something is wrong. Once that happens, we can't hear the voice even if it's screaming.

When I was in grade school, I thought what the other kids did was, for the most part, stupid. I couldn't tell you why I thought it was stupid except that I thought it was petty and boring.

Needless to say, I was not very popular in grade school.

I tell you this because, even at a young age, I felt different. I saw things differently. I would excel at some work and fail miserably at other work. Adults told me that I just wasn't applying myself. As a result, very little was expected of me. By my twenties, I was adrift in a world that seemed like it had no place for me. Try as I might, nothing fit. Whenever I was asked to create something, my ideas were so big they were impossible to achieve in that setting and with my skills. I appeared impractical. I could not get comfortable with the idea of a regular job and, for a while, it was hard for me to keep one. The inside and the outside of my life never seemed to match. I was frustrated and unhappy. I had such big dreams and next to nothing to show for it.

Since then, seen in hindsight, I have been able to put my earlier experiences into context. Now my experiences seem like a perfect plan and my dissatisfaction - instead of causing me to distance myself from others - is used to fuel my creativity.

"The dissatisfaction with what exists is sometimes the first step toward something different".

Seen in the context of the above quote, visionaries can be seen as dissatisfied people. As has been said, "There is a crack in everything - that's how the light gets in." But until the visionary understands this, their dissatisfaction will remain meaningless.

Sometimes, instead of hearing the call, a person might just be overcome by discomfort and unhappiness. This unfulfilled impulse to create shows up as depression, anxiety, or a tugging feeling in the back of the person's mind. Maybe it pushes the affected person from one place to another (or from one job to another) seeking something they can't quite put their finger on - and if only they could find it, they would be happy.

Sometimes, the visionary feels like a stranger in a strange land, where no one seems to be thinking like they are, and wondering whether there's anyone else who thinks remotely like they do - someone who can make their vision happen. Once visionaries manifest their visions, they can finally understand their capacity for change and transition. And while others may someday reap the rewards of your efforts and the efforts of others like you, you will need to be always on the edge - pushing for what has not yet come into being.

It is my guess that if you are reading this guide, then you already have a sense of who you are and what work you want to do. If this is the case then chances are you connected to something in this section that confirmed what you have already begun to know and believe for yourself. If for some reason this is not the case, see how and what words, and phrases tug at your awareness and help you to connect to your own inner calling or go to the Troubleshooting section of this guide to clarify what is holding you back.

Whatever it is that you feel passionately about, you can do it! You were meant to do that thing more than anything else. Think about yourself in the terms that Alan Watts used: "You are the perfect expression of the universe exactly where you are in this moment." Or, as Ralph Waldo Emerson wrote: "The eye was placed where one ray should fall, that it might testify of that particular ray."

When you begin to see yourself as a being who is connected organically to the rest of the world - whose personal wants are whispers of the universe - then you can begin to see your work as imperative, but less personally driven. Of course, because we are doing exactly what we want to do, we benefit as well. Following what you love and exploring the ideas and options that emerge is a great way to hone your ability to envision a different future for yourself and others.

What you need to know is:

You are the one you're looking for.

You are the one that you have been waiting for.

What you want is yours to create.

Nothing extra is necessary to achieve your vision.

You have all you need within yourself.

Making Your Vision a Reality

Vision

So what is meant by the term "vision"?

It's simple. Whatever difference you want to make in the world - ending hunger and war, teaching parents how to raise children better, teaching partners how to love better, or however you want to make the world a better place - it is important to have a clear, desired end result. Your vision is your all-encompassing goal. You might never ultimately achieve this goal on your own - For example ending world hunger is a pretty tall order - but your contribution will get the world closer to that goal.

In order to get you going as quickly as possible, I am going to have you start right away with trying to get a sense of your vision. If you have difficulty doing this, don't worry. The "Trouble Shooting" section later in this book is designed to help you. If you are already clear about what your problem is (or you are absolutely stuck) you might want to move on to a later section right away. Otherwise, try the first two tools and take your first step.

Your first step is to create your Vision Statement. Most businesses use this step, as well, to help them formulate their business plan and it's a good way to help clarify your project. Here's an exercise to help you write your Vision Statement:

Tool #1: Your Vision
Ask yourself the following:

What I want to change about the world is:

One to three things that I think the world needs are:

What I want to communicate to the world is:

I want to help or serve:

How I want to help or serve the world is:

The kind of difference I want to make in the world is:

Now, write a statement of up to three sentences that encapsulates your vision - your Vision Statement. If you have more than one vision as a result of this exercise, pay attention to whether your multiple visions fit into one larger category. Remember, your vision can be BIG.

Here are some examples:
To end hunger
To live in a world that is free from violence
To clothe the people of Vermont
To teach the girls of rural Massachusetts that they are powerful

My Visions Statement is:

Your Mission

Your vision is something you may never fully achieve by yourself. It might not even be achieved in your lifetime. But what role will you play in bringing your vision one step closer to reality? This role then becomes your mission - your unique part in creating this vision. The next step is determining what exactly you plan to do.

Many times a person can see more than one way they might work toward their vision. If this is the case, don't worry about it now. See the "Overwhelmed?" part of the "Trouble Shooting" section.

If you are ready to move forward, here are some examples:

To constantly strive to meet or exceed our customer needs and expectations of price, service, and selection. To this end, we will perform periodic reviews of the marketplace to improve our offerings.

Our Mission is to promote the value of learning, self-worth among students and staff, quality performance among students and staff, and transition for students to productive and responsible participation in society.

To provide millions of Indians a comfortable, safe & affordable home - and a reason to smile! - Rajeev Khurana

PANPHA represents over 320 non-profit providers of long-term care and housing services for 65,000 elderly residents across Pennsylvania. The Association is committed to helping its members provide quality care efficiently and effectively for the individuals and families they serve. In an age of impersonal care, PANPHA members put people before profits.

"Provide affordable, educational, and outdoor recreational activities in a safe, clean, and inviting environment for people of all ages through sound business and management practices.

Tool #2: Your Mission
Complete these statements.

I am good at:

I love to:

I am interested in:

I have had prior success when:

I see myself personally contributing to my vision by:

Where to Start: Values and Goals

Once you are clear on your mission and vision, you need to create a plan to achieve them. To start, you need two pieces - "values" and "goals."

Goals are the end results you are trying to achieve. They are the "what" in your plan. Values are the "how" of the plan. To understand the difference, here's an example. Business ventures are designed to make money. A goal might be to achieve a certain level of sales or amount of money, similar to any other business designed to make money. However, any two businesses might have drastically different values. One might value respect and sustainability. The other might value speed of return on investments. The way each business or project reaches its goals is influenced by individual and company values.

Values

Often, visionaries are discouraged by the lack of similarity between their own values and those implicit in a "standard business plan." And if they ask for help, they are often unhappy about the type of help they receive. This does not have to be the case, and, for your plan right now, it will not be the case. Values are key to the visionary's plan - and its success. Values help visionaries create plans as well as help them make the decisions they need to make to move that plan forward.

Here are a couple of examples of values from my organizations:

Example 1: Non-profit developed to stop gender-based violence.

Empowerment: We seek to empower all people at every level of the organization and its programs.
Awareness: Our organization's goal is to educate others about the nuances of women's leadership and gender-based violence.
Effectiveness: Our programs and methods are successful at empowering women and decreasing gender-based violence.
Sustainability: Our program and its systems are designed to be balanced and harmonious.

Example 2: Therapy Group

Client-centered: We listen to each client's individual needs and provide for those needs.

Holistic: We effectively treat each client's symptoms while never losing sight of the whole person.

Grounded: We choose quality and knowledgeable practitioners of effective disciplines.

Balanced: We carefully balance the art and science of healing.

Available: We offer extended hours and multiple practitioners for client convenience.

Effective: We craft treatment programs that pay attention to the most relevant treatment, including complementary and supportive alternatives.

Compassionate: We maintain strong, supportive relationships with our clients.

Tool #3: Value Sheet

Make a list of values that you and/or your project will use while acting and interacting. Then, write a short phrase that describes these values. If you are not sure, think of some values that are important to you in everyday life. It is likely that these values will also be used in your business. Also, here is a short list of some common values:

Abundance	Fairness
Acceptance	Flexibility
Adaptability	Giving
Altruism	Honesty
Awareness	Intelligence
Balance	Joy
Bravery	Knowledge
Charity	Leadership
Clarity	Open-mindedness
Congruency	Originality
Consistency	Philanthropy
Cooperation	Pragmatism
Creativity	Recognition
Decisiveness	Refinement
Devotion	Skillfulness
Economy	Spirituality
Efficiency	Synergy
Empathy	Thoroughness
Enjoyment	Vision
Expertise	Wisdom
Expressiveness	

1.

2.

3.

4.

5.

6.

7.

8.

9.

10.

Put a star next to your top three values. Remember values are how you will make your decisions and reach your goals. If you are having a difficult time making a decision about something return to your values to help yourself get clear about what is important.

Goals

Long-Term Goals

A clear goal requires the ability to step outside the current circumstances and look at the larger picture. In order to set appropriate goals, make sure you are aware of your mission and vision before you set them. Having the wrong goal for your project, or even having goals that are slightly off the mark, will make the work of getting what you want to get accomplished much harder - meaning it will take that much more time. Perhaps your goal is to feed 100 people a month or to decrease the number of women on welfare by providing jobs with decent wages. In order for them to be workable goals you need to make sure that they are clear, measurable, and that they outline the specifics of your mission.

Tool #4: Goal Sheet

If you achieve your objectives, what will you have accomplished? These are your big goals. List 3-10 long-term goals.

Goal	Definition
1.	
2.	
3.	
4.	
5.	
6.	
7.	
8.	
9.	
10.	

Your Business or Project Plan

Now that you know your goals and values, you will need to create the beginning of your plan - your plan is comprised of the tinier goals and actions that will eventually achieve the larger goals, actions, and eventually your mission.

To make your Plan, you will need to think about your long-term goals. You will soon realize that these long-term goals are actually comprised of several short-term goals, and these will be the "Steps" of your Plan.

Breaking down your long-term goals is one of the more challenging parts of creating your plan, and is frequently a point where people get overwhelmed. There are different ways to figure this out, but I find that many non-linear thinkers like the following technique to get them started.

Tool #5: Create a Mind Map

A Mind Map is a visual representation of your goals and what is needed to accomplish them. The process of making a Mind Map will allow you to see your project from a different perspective. This perspective, in and of itself, will be helpful. It is likely that you will realize there are connections between things that you did not see before - or even the reverse -: you may begin to see the differences between things that you thought were similar.

Follow these instructions by Illumine Training to create your mind map.

1. Take a blank piece of paper, A4 or larger. Blank paper allows 360º of freedom to express the full range of your cortical skills, whereas pre-drawn lines restrict the natural flow of your thoughts.

2. Use the paper in landscape orientation. Words and images have more space in the direction we write, so they don't bump into margins as quickly.

3. Start in the center. Thoughts start in the center of our mental world. The Mind Map page reflects this!

4. Make a central image that represents the topic about which you are writing/thinking. Remember these tips to make your image more impactful:

   a) A picture is worth a thousand words. It opens up associations, focuses the thoughts, is fun and results in better recall.
   a) Use at least three colors. Colors stimulate the right cortical activity of imagination as well as capturing and holding attention.
   b) Keep the height and width of the central image to approximately 2" or 5cm (proportionately larger for bigger paper). This size gives plenty of space for the rest of your Mind Map, while making it large enough to be the clear focus of the topic.
   c) Allow the image to create its own shape (do not use a frame). The unique shape makes it more memorable and enjoyable. A frame makes the center a monotony of shape and disconnects the branches.

5.The main themes around the central image are like the chapter headings of a book:

   a) Print this word in CAPITALS or draw an image.
   b) Place on a line of the same length.
   c) The central lines are thick, curved and organic, i.e. like your arm joining your body, or the branch of a tree to the trunk.
   d) Connect directly to the central image.

e) The main themes, connected to the central image on the main branches, allow their relative importance to be seen. These are the Basic Ordering Ideas (BOIs) and aggregate and focus the rest of the Mind Map.

f) Printing (versus cursive) allows the brain to photograph the image, thus giving easier reading and more immediate recall.

g) Word length equals line length. An extra line disconnects thoughts; length accentuates the connection.

h) Curved lines give visual rhythm and variety and so are easier to remember, more pleasant to draw and less boring to look at. Thicker central lines show relative importance.

i) Connected to the image because the brain works by association not separated, disconnected lines.

6. Start to add a second level of thought. These words or images are linked to the main branch that triggered them.

Remember:

a) Connecting lines are thinner.

b) Words are still printed but may be lower case.

c) Your initial words and images stimulate associations. Attach whatever word or image is triggered. Allow the random movement of your thought; you do not have to 'finish' one branch before moving on.

d) Connected lines create relationships and a structure. They also demonstrate the level of importance, as from a branch to a twig.

e) The size and style of the letters provide additional data about the importance and meaning of the word/image.

7. Add a third or fourth level of data as thoughts come to you:

a) Use images as much as you can, instead of - or in addition to - the words.

b) Allow your thoughts to come freely, meaning you 'jump about' the Mind Map as the links and associations occur to you.

c) Your brain is like a multi-handed thought-ball catcher. The Mind Map allows you to catch and keep whatever 'thought ball' is thrown by your brain.

8. Add a new dimension to your Mind Map. Boxes add depth around the word or image to make some important points stand out.

9. Sometimes enclose branches of a Mind Map with outlines in color:

a) Enclose the shape of the branch and hug the shape tightly.

b) Use different colors and styles.

c) The outlines will create unique shapes as you find in clouds and will aid your memory.

d) These provide immediate visual linking. They can also encourage follow-up and remind you of action you need to take.

e) They can also show connection between branches by using the same color outline.

10. Make each Mind Map a little more beautiful, artistic, colorful, imaginative and dimensional. Your eyes and brain will be attracted to your Mind Map:

a) It will be easier to remember.

b) It will be more attractive to you (and to others as well).

11. Have fun!

Add a little humor, exaggeration or absurdity wherever you can. Your brain will delight in getting the maximum use and enjoyment from this process and will, therefore, learn faster, recall more effectively and think more clearly.

Mind Map

Tool #6: Short-term Goals

At this point in time, you have a vision, a mission, a list of goals, and a Mind Map. In order to create your plan you will need to begin to organize the short-term goals that you can see on your Mind Map. Short-term goals are goals that can be completed within one year. Short-term goals ultimately lead to your long-term goals. When creating your short-term goals, make them specific, measurable, action oriented and timely. Some of the ways to decide this are to ask yourself:

Does this need to get done in order for me to accomplish other goals?
Is this likely to have the strongest positive effect if I do it?
Is this likely to have a strong negative effect if I do not do it?
Is this essential to my end goal and must it always be a focus?

Put your goals in their order of importance and put a date by each goal for when it is best accomplished by. Remember that if it is high on the list it should also have a closer completion date. Don't worry about being exact with this. It is just basic organization of your ideas so that really important things do not get lost and not-so-important things do not get all your attention:

List of goals in order of importance and with dates:

1.

2.

3.

4.

5.

6.

7.

8.

9.

10.

The previous tools (Tools 3-6) provide you with the skeleton of your plan. Using these, you will be able to create the structure that holds your dream together. Don't be concerned that you have forgotten an important aspect or lack an important piece of the puzzle. You can return to these tools at any time to clarify or adjust your plan.

To begin to develop your plan, look at your list of goals that you derived from creating your Mind Map. Each one of these goals will require that you take a number of steps to achieve it. Some people find it helpful to use the next tool to figure out what the steps are that will ultimately have them reach their short-term goal.

Tool #7: Short-term Goal Development: Working Backwards

Write a goal down on the right-hand side of this page. To the left of it, write what you need in order to make that goal happen. To the right of that, write what you need in order to have that happen. Keep doing this exercise until you find that you have what you need. Do this with each of your goals. If you look at the example below you will see that working backwards from what you ultimately want provides you with insight into the steps that it will take to make it happen.

Example

Step #1 <business marketing materials

Step #2 <designer<business marketing materials

Step #3 <contact potential designers <designer<business marketing materials

Step #4 <research designers<contact potential designers<designer<business marketing materials

Step #5 <create content <research designers<contact designers<designer<business marketing materials

Short-Term Goals to Action Steps

To bring your plan closer to reality, you will need to take your short-term goals and turn them into action steps. You have already begun to take steps in this direction by making your Mind Map and completing Tool #7. Tool #8 takes this to the next level by bring your short term goals into the present via action steps.

Tool #8: Working Forward

Take your work from Tool #7. Start on the left-hand side this time. Ask yourself, "What do I need to do to get myself to the next step?" Repeat this question until you have explored all the options or have found a step that you are satisfied with. Then, define this goal. What exactly do you need to do? Call someone? Take a class? Do research? How will you know that you have done it? What will you have by the time you are done - information, permissions, another question? Is it something that you can do?

You will not move your plan forward if your goals are to wait for other people to do things. When are you to accomplish this - tomorrow, next week, next month?

Tool #9: Action Steps

What can you do now? Look at the work that you have done on your short-term goals. What on the list can you start working on right away? Take these actions and put them into a planner. What will you work on today, tomorrow, or for the rest of the week?

Tool #10: Weekly Re-Assessment

Assess your short-term goals and actions weekly, if not daily. In order to keep yourself on track, you must continue to look at your plan and figure out what action steps can be taken as well as revise any areas that have changed due to new information.

Heart-Centered Strategy/
Remember Your Values

It is not enough just to be able to plan. In order to bring something truly visionary into being, you will also need to pay attention each step of the way to whether you are adhering to your values. It is important that every action step that you take, every person that you interact with, and every goal that you reach upholds the values that you are committed to.

Tool #11: In this Moment

Go back to Tool #3 - your Value Sheet. Write a statement about what you can do right now to make each value a part of what you are doing. Write these statements below and then write and hang these statements in a place you will frequently see them.

Tool #12: Negative Beliefs

Sometimes we have really good intentions, but when it comes right down to it, we don't really believe that that is the way the world works. These negative beliefs prevent us from seeing opportunities and also stop us from truly acting from our values. Take a moment to write out all of your doubts, fears, and negative predictions about how the world works on one half of a sheet of paper. Then, rephrase each belief to something more positive, yet still fully believable.

Your Plan is Complete

At this point, as a result of completing the "Making Your Vision a Reality" part of the guide, you should have completed your plan. You should have a clear sense of where you are going and how to get there. You should also be locked on to the values that are most important to making your vision complete.

Tool #13: Take Stock

Assess the process so far. Try going back to a part of this guide and re-doing an exercise every day if you are unclear. Or contact a life/business coach and get some professional help. You will likely not need many sessions - likely just a couple - to figure out where the problem is. Make sure to send your life/business coach the work that you have done so far; this will make it possible for your coach to better support you.

What have you learned from this process?

Are there areas where you are clearer?

Are there areas that you feel are unclear?

Troubleshooting

If you need more help clarifying your vision or figuring out what your role is in the unfolding of your mission, read the following sections for some additional tools to help you figure it out. If you are feeling really confident about your mission and vision work, you might want to skip ahead to the "Common Obstacles" section.

Confused?

What if you hear the call but don't know what to make of it? Maybe you feel that people are disconnected and you want to create more connection. Does that mean you become a social worker or start a blog? How do you know what form your efforts should take?

I wish I could say, "Well, all you have to do is _____." But it is not that simple. When you are building from an intuitive place - and a lot of visionaries are - sometimes you have to wait for the vision to become clearer to even be able to start on your plan. If you just have not gotten clear about what your mission or vision is, there are some things you can do to move the process along.

Tool #14: Describe What You Love
Within what you love are clues to the unfolding of your larger vision. For example:

Environments you love:

People you love to be around:

Types of tasks that you love:

When you like to get up or go to sleep:

Books you love to read:

Causes you are inspired by:

People you are inspired by:

What you do for fun:

What you look forward to more than anything else:

If you don't know, then anything that you are drawn to or fascinated by may be the clue you're looking for. Make lists of anything and everything that you love - from objects to activities. Make sure there are at least 20 things on the list.

1.

2.

3.

4.

5.

6.

7.

8.

9.

10.

11.

12.

13.

14.

15.

16.

17.

18.

19.

20.

Tool #15: Preferences as they Might Relate to Vocation

Look at your list of loves; these are the "What's" – the "what" you are interested in. Try to be objective and describe your preferences. For example, I prefer being able to spend lots of time outside and interacting with only a few people. I prefer freedom in my schedule so that I can travel. Then, ask yourself "how much" questions such as:

How much do you like to be with other people?
How much do you like to work?
How much do you like to not work?
How much do you like to travel?

Write your list of preferences:

1.

2.

3.

4.

5.

6.

7.

8.

9.

10.

Tool #16: Your Dissatisfaction

Are you both dissatisfied and confused? Pay attention to your dissatisfaction. Within this dissatisfaction is the nucleus of what you want to create.

Spend five minutes writing a list - or free writing - about your dissatisfaction. Then, go to your list of loves and preferences. These are the likely ingredients, components, actions, and potential forms and methods you might like to use. While looking at all of them, let them come together in your mind. What options appear? Brainstorm. After you have reviewed the information found on those lists, try free-writing until a form starts to emerge.

Tool #17: Contemplation

Don't do anything: spend time every day in contemplation. Ask the question, "What is my life's work?" and then spend time breathing and connecting to your body and your environment.

Overwhelmed?

Some visionaries have the opposite problem. Instead of feeling like they don't know at all what to do, they feel like there are a million things they would love to do. So they flit around from one idea to the next, never getting traction and never really moving forward. Personally, I can't look at a "for lease" space in a city without imagining what type of business might do well in it. Every time I hear of someone planning to sell their business, I start to think of what I might do with it in their place.

Does this sound like you? Many creative people find that it does. Most need to develop skills that allow them to see the difference between the many (sometimes random) thoughts of their beautiful, active imaginations and the ideas on which they really want to act. For some, help can be found in Attention Deficit Disorder (ADD) books like Driven to Distraction.

There are two main pieces to making this work. The first is knowing what you love the most - that way you have a clear sense of where your priorities are. The second has to do with where your skills can be best used. If you have not used Tool #14, go back and use it now to determine what it is that you truly love as it relates to the work you might do in the world.

Tool #18: Reality Check #1

If you are seriously considering a venture, list the main components of what that venture would require. If you are uncertain, try to find someone who knows (or some venture that is similar) and then make the list. Check that list against the list you created in Tool #15.

How close are these two lists? What can you learn from this?

Tool #19: Reality Check #2

What are your skills? What do you bring to the table? How does the list of your skills compare to what the venture requires? If you are someone who comes up with lots of ideas, you can use this process of comparing the venture to what you love and then to what you can easily do as a way to objectively determine if you should invest your time and energy in the project about which you are fantasizing. In time, this becomes second nature, making it easy to determine where you would like to concentrate your efforts.

My Skills are:

Tool #20: Give Them Away

If you truly are the generator of many ideas, perhaps you can develop a habit of giving them away to people who are likely to see them as their life's work. That way, everyone wins. Think of people who might really benefit from your ideas. List them below and tell them about your ideas as soon as you are able.

My fabulous give away ideas are:

Tool #21: Stop Trying to Figure it Out

Spend time every day in quiet contemplation. Ask the question, "What would I find most satisfying?" and then spend time breathing and connecting to your body and your environment.

Stuck

Sometimes people are afraid of making choices because they fear that the result might be that they get stuck doing something that brings them absolutely no joy. They shudder at the idea of becoming another unhappy person - or unhappy with themselves as a person. They would rather remain immobilized than risk this outcome.

Time after time, I see this happen with very talented and sensitive people. It is as if they overuse their talent and their sensitivity. Instead of using it for their work, they use it for analysing all the potential outcomes from the perspective of never having started. The thinking looks something like: if I continue to act the way that I do, but situations around me magically change, then I will be unhappy; I can't bear that. Meanwhile, they are unhappy with their lives as they are. What is missing here is the awareness that they are in charge of what they choose, accept, and act upon.

Others are afraid of the possibilities suggested by their future. James Hillman tells a great story about a famous bull-fighter. The bullfighter spent his first 12 years tied to his mother's apron strings. Hillman suggests that the bullfighter was, on some level, aware of his future and was spending as much time as possible in the safety of his mother's apron. Some people might feel their potential greatness and shiver at the risk that is implied by it - whether successful or not. If you can see where you want to be, then all you have to do is take one tiny step in that direction. If you keep doing that, you will eventually get to where you want to be. Not only that, but you will gain confidence along the way. The process is just as important as - perhaps more important than - the destination.

Tool #22: One Action per Day

Think of one small thing that you can do each day that moves you in the direction of doing the work that you really want to do. But PAY ATTENTION to how it might relate to your calling. Make sure to do something you LOVE doing and do it daily. Use Tool #14 if you are not clear about where to start. Remember, do it daily!

My one action per day is:

Tool #23: Stop Your Mind

Spend time each day in quiet contemplation. Ask yourself, "Could I ever be truly content and not live out my life's purpose?"

Is it too Late?

Perhaps you have been telling yourself that you have missed your chance - that, at this point, you will never be good enough to succeed at your goal. Julia Cameron answers this predicament though the following short story.
There is a sixty-year-old woman who has always wanted to play the piano. When asked why she does not start learning, she says, "Do you know how old I will be when I finally learn?" The reply was, "The same age you will be if you don't." Moral: it is never too late. If you really want to do something, start today.

Tool #24: Where Will You be if You Try?

Make a list of what you have not been doing because you have been using the excuse that you are "out of time." For each thing, answer these questions:

How good are you at this now?
How good would you be if you worked toward this goal for five years?
How good would you be if you worked toward this goal for ten years?
How good will you be if you do not do anything?

Not Good Enough?

People who suffer from chronic low self-esteem have a very difficult time imagining their dreams becoming reality. They so deeply believe that they are not good enough that they don't even try. They cannot see their skills, talents, and abilities. If you believed this completely, however, you would not even read this guide. But if you believe this partially and you know it is holding you back - try the following.

Tool #25: Ask a Friend

Ask three close friends to share with you what they see as your strengths and your talents. Ask all three to both write it down and say it directly to you. Don't have them read what they wrote and don't take notes while they talk. Have them make the list and then have them sit down, look you in the eye, and tell you what they think.

Then, be honest with yourself. It is entirely possible that your strengths and weaknesses don't mesh well with your goals. In order to make things happen, it is important to be firmly grounded in reality - not erring on the side of being either worthless or grand. This is especially true when it comes to certain specific jobs when there are a limited number of available positions.

Say you want to be a Harvard Professor of Philosophy. But you have no connections. You have never been to college. You are 75 years old and English is your second language, which you just started to learn last year (kudos, by the way). Chances are, you are not going to be a Harvard Professor of Philosophy in this lifetime. Right? Right. However, those facts should not stop you from studying, writing, and talking about philosophy. And there are many other things that you might be able to do that are related to philosophy (or even Harvard) that would be really satisfying.

We can create a lot of confusion and pain when we fixate on the form we feel our vision should take. In the previous example, the love of philosophy is the driving force behind the vision and the Harvard Professorship is just the (probably unattainable) form. When we come from this place of being fixated on a narrow goal, we are frequently not coming from our own essence and what truly and deeply makes us happy.

Tool #26: Process, Not Product

Write down the things that you want to achieve, but think are out of reach. This will help you figure out what it is that you love about the doing of the goal - not the achieving of the goal.

If I am Still Not Clear

At this point, you should be a little bit loosened up. You should have your vision and should have started to work at the blocks that hold you back from seeing your role in creating the vision. If you are still not clear about either your vision or your mission, this might be a good time to set up some sessions with a life coach. Four sessions should be enough - if you have thoroughly worked through this section of the guide - to get clarity about what your calling is.

Common Obstacles

Money

Very frequently, people put money between themselves and whatever it is that they want to do. I am not going to tell you that money does not make a difference - it does. Having the capital to develop your plan and take the action that needs to be taken makes some decisions and even whole projects much easier.

However, do not be fooled into thinking that money is the make-or-break factor in your plan. More often than not, passion and ingenuity can triumph over some of the most difficult situations. Sometimes, if you have a very large problem with money, you might even need to do some work around it before beginning work on your plan. See Rich Dad, Poor Dad in the Reference section of this guide.

When what you are bringing into the world is needed, what you need to make it happen inevitably becomes available. This is true with money as well. Have faith that, if you begin to move in the direction of your ultimate goal, things will shift and the way will be clearer. Don't give up.

Tool #27: Negative Beliefs about Money

In case you did not list "money" when creating your list of negative beliefs in Tool #12, think about it now and write down your negative beliefs about money. Then, rephrase these beliefs to be more positive - yet still believable. If you find that you are particularly negative about money, you might want to write down your positive beliefs and reread them daily for a time. Without changing these beliefs, your chances at success will be limited.

My negative beliefs about money are:

If you need capital, and it is likely you do, you will need to think of some clever ways to bring it into your life. Business people will frequently tell you that they took some big risks because they believed that what they were trying to do was going to be successful. However, they will also tell you that it was not always successful. It is important to realize that just because you believe in your idea does not mean it is guaranteed to succeed. But, if you do not believe in your idea, it does not have a chance. If you are concerned about the viability of your project, it makes sense to hire someone to do a market analysis. It will be well worth the investment to see on paper the viability of what you are planning.

Tool #28: Sources of Money

Think of anybody and everybody who might be willing to support your venture. This should include friends, family, institutions, as well as friends of friends and friends of family.

Make a list of potential investors:

Tool #29: What Can You Do for Free?

Like I said before, do not get too hung up on the money. Usually there are myriad steps you can take without spending a dime. Of course, this likely means you will be spending your time, but hopefully you have one if you do not have the other. A great resource for this is the Guerilla Marketing Series. This series tells you about many low-cost and free marketing options.

Make a list of the things that you can do to create and promote your business for free or close to free:

Here are some hints:

Post on social media
Tell family and friends
Network with colleagues
Research
Trade with other professionals for services
Donate your time (don't overdo it)

Time

Next to money, time is definitely the next most commonly used reason for not being able to move a plan forward. There just never seems to be enough time to do what we truly want to do. Sometimes our lives are so full that finding time is truly an obstacle.

In order to see how much time plays a role in stopping your plan, use the following tool.

Tool #30: Filling Your Schedule

Make a list of everything you need to do in a week as well as how many hours it takes to do each thing, remembering to add 56 hours for sleeping and 21 for eating. Add them all up and then subtract the result from 168 (the number of hours in a week). The result is your leftover hours each week - how much time you have to spare for your project. If the result is at zero or less than zero, decide if any of the activities you listed might be taken out or modified to create more time. If not, you probably don't have any time to add a new project.

How much time do I have for my project:
168-(56-21)=91 - your other activities = your project time.

Depending on your situation, you may need to make difficult choices about when to work on your plan and when you need to tend to other aspects of your life - such as survival. This just makes your plan a little different. You might need to adjust your timetable or invest time in finding people with the money to support your plan.

Tool #31: Prioritize

One of the habits of a highly effective person taken from the book Seven Habits of Highly Effective People is Prioritizing. Without priorities our plans just never seem to move forward and our lives feel cluttered and less exciting. Now that you have established your Mission, Vision and Goals, it is important that you figure out what is most essential to your forward movement. The way to figure this out is to ask, "What is it that needs to get done in order to have the rest of my plan/life be successful?"

My priorities at this time are:

    1.

    2.

    3.

Tool #32: Get a Planner

If you think that planners are for boring people or business people or boring business people, it is time to change your view. Your planner is an essential tool to your success. I highly suggest that you check out Planner Pads. (See the resources section. They are great tools that come with a CD on how to most effectively use them.

I will repeat: a planner is an essential tool for your success. You will want to use your planner like this: Check your planner at least once every day and update it every week. This means at the beginning of the week you sit down, look at what you did the week before and map out what you need to do the next week. If you schedule time blocks to work on projects, these are not optional. Treat them like you are going to work for someone else. Show up on time ready to get the job done. Everyday - in the morning, preferably - check your planner to figure out what you need to get done for the day. Make sure to prioritize what is important. Check out Dave Allen's Getting Things Done to learn about time management from a master.

Tool #33: What is Taking Your Time That is Not Important

If you do not have enough time in your week or you fill out your schedule and have your project scheduled but do not seem to ever get your project moving, ask yourself what is taking your time that is not important. See if you can eliminate these things from your schedule. If you cannot eliminate them then try to reduce the time spent on them as much as possible.

These are the things that are wasting my time:

Support

If you are a person who has come to the erroneous conclusion that you should already have the answers - or if you're feeling discouraged because you can't seem to figure out the answers to your current situation on your own - then this section is for you.

Not having the right support can definitely make a plan more difficult to complete. It is not ALWAYS possible to see what you should do - whether your life is in balance or whether you are on target with your business idea. It is also not possible to get the job done by yourself. Without support, your project is likely to wither.

Make sure that you have people around you who can support you in every part of your work. This might be a friend who nurtures and supports you no matter what, a colleague who shares visions with you, a lawyer who ensures your legal safety, or a coach who keeps you focused and moving forward. These people all know something you do not. You can spend a lot of time trying to figure it out or you can save time by putting the right person on the job from the beginning.

Sometimes, it is not about getting the job done - it is about knowing someone has your back. It is harder to complete any plan if you are lacking people who believe in you and your project's potential. There will be moments when you feel overwhelmed and maybe even want to quit. The supportive people in your life will keep you going.

Tool #34: Pick Your Team

Make a list of the people you know are on your side. This list can be as long as you want it to be. Write the person's name and then the type of support that they are able to give you. Keep this list handy. Sometimes people forget who might be able to help them once they need help.

These are the members of my team:

Tool #35: Pick Your Imaginary Team

OK, so, as much as we might need it, sometimes the people that we know are not able to give us all the support that we need. Because of this, it is helpful to have an imaginary support team. Make a list of all the people you would like to have at your back and why you would like to have them there. Know that, when the in-the-flesh help is not there, the imaginary support team can never fail you. If you find yourself in a moment without support, use your imagination. Ask one or all of your imaginary team members what they would do in this situation. You might be surprised by what fresh perspective this brings.

These are the members of my imaginary team:

Tool #36: Professional Support

As I said before, the fastest and best way to move forward is to have the right support. If you are starting up a business, you will want to have both professional and personal support. In case you did not list your professional support under Tool #21, now is your chance to do it. However, unless you feel very confident in your abilities, I would suggest getting professional help with the following areas:

Design: Most industries are highly competitive. To set yourself apart from the competition, it pays to have a designer work on your marketing materials and Website.

Bookkeeping and accounting: While it might be possible to keep your own books using a program like QuickBooks®, a couple of hours with a professional may be a bigger help. Unless you are great with numbers, an accountant for your business will be more than worth the cost. While it might save you a couple hundred dollars a year to maintain your books yourself, it could cost you much more if you make a mistake.

Legal issues: You definitely want to consult a lawyer before signing any contracts or entering into any business agreements. If you do not think that you can afford this type of help, then I suggest going to the SBA to see if there are any lawyers in the area who work pro bono for a good cause.

Business Development: From writing a business plan to getting a business coach, you can move faster and more easily by getting this type of support.

Write in the names of any professional support you already have in place. Add in the type of professional support that you will need to seek out. Also, see Start Up Basics to make sure you have the essentials on your list.

This is my professional support team:

Fear

Inevitably, when people attempt to reach for their dreams, they hit a wall of fear. When asked about it, they might say things like: "I am afraid that I will fail," or, "What I want comes at too high of a price."
Fear is a normal response to change. But instead of thinking that fear is a sign that you are doing something wrong, try finding ways of acknowledging your fears and persisting in the face of them. If you are uncertain how to do that, try some of these ideas:

Tool #37: How do I Respond to Fear?

Pay attention to how you respond to feeling fear. Fear can be sneaky. It can show up as confusion, anger, and/or apathy. Sometimes a person will not identify their feeling as fear, but as another emotion. Learn your own habits and this awareness will help you move forward.

When I am afraid I:

Tool #38: What is at risk?

If you set a goal and then find that you are not moving toward it, look for how you might be afraid of either achieving or not achieving the outcome. This question can also point to beliefs or contracts that a person has made with himself or others. What is the perceived or emotional risk in moving forward?

If I move forward, then:

Tool #39: Take Care of Yourself.

This step appears again and again when it comes to reaching our goals. It is based on the idea that we should not do harm to ourselves. If the situation feels risky, find a way to give yourself some security. It is important that we stretch toward our goals and it is important that we don't break.

When I feel afraid, what are five things I can do to take care of myself?

1.
2.
3.
4.
5.

Tool #40: Fake It 'til You Make It

Ask yourself, "How would I act if I was not afraid?" This solution may sound a bit simplistic, but it can also be effective. If you do not have the answer to this question, then look around for someone who seems like they might, and try their answer on for size.

If I was not afraid, I would:

All in all, remember to keep your eye on your goal. Fear can be a sign that you really want something. It is much easier to find the strength to achieve your goal if you are really locked in on how important it is to you. This can help you deal with the discomfort instilled by fear.

Knowledge/Skills

The other thing that holds us back is a lack of knowledge. While this book is designed to give people core pieces of knowledge that might help them succeed, I want to touch on this as a topic in and of itself. Creating a business, project, or heart-centered vision is learning a new skill or set of skills. We learn from trial and error and we learn from others who have gone before us. The more you learn what you do not know, the easier you can make it on yourself. If you feel like you are missing a key piece of information, do some research and find someone who can help you move forward.

Tool #41: There is Always Someone Who Knows the Answer

What knowledge or skills do you know that you need from someone else:

There are a couple of skills that, if you do not have them, will become obstacles to your being able to succeed - organization and communication. I cover some very key points in these next several paragraphs but I highly recommend developing these skills in yourself or partnering with someone who has these skills if you do not.

The Skill of Organization

The bottom line is that your plan is not going to work without organization. The more time pressures you have, the more important it is that you are well organized - even at the beginning. Organization, in many ways, equals success. Despite what is sometimes implied, there is no one way for every person to stay organized; however, there are some golden rules:

Write it down. Get it out of your head and down onto paper or into your organizer. A full head equals lots of stress and less efficiency.

Have it handy. Keep this up-to-date list of what needs to be done next on-hand at all times. Unless you are organized, you will not recognize the many times available to you to take action on these next steps.

Prioritize. Make sure that you do things in the order of "most important" to "least important." Avoid getting hung up on the little details or making decisions emotionally rather than rationally.

Focus. Don't do something if it does not need to be done. In other words, if it is efficient to check your email twice per day, do not check it three times a day. That additional time is wasted time.

For more information on organization, see Getting Things Done in the Reference section of this guide. If you have a really difficult time getting organized - for example, if you have ADD - then I suggest that you seek out professional help. Not having this type of help can make it impossible for someone with ADD or other problems with organization to be successful.

Tool #42: Learn How to Organize

Read a book or hire a professional. You can even ask a friend who is particularly capable in this way. But, make sure that you do it.

This is how I plan to improve my organization:

Communication

No matter what it is that you want to do, it will almost certainly require that you are able to communicate with others to make it happen. Unfortunately, many people grow into adults not knowing the basics of how to communicate effectively. The book People Skills which you can find in the reference section, is a great introduction to these skills.

Tool #43: Watch a Master

One of the best ways to learn how to communicate well is to watch someone who is very good at it. This first-hand experience of good communication is the fastest and best way to learn communication skills. The most important skill in communication isn't talking - it's listening. Listening is the key to determining what is actually happening in the communication. After people learn their initial listening skills - such as "do not interrupt" and "make sure that you have understood the other person before responding" - the challenge comes in when there is some sort of conflict. Once strong emotions or beliefs enter the picture, a person is more inclined to assert his beliefs and opinions rather than deeply listen to the other person. If you find that this is happening, it is best to take a few breaths and ask the other person for a moment. Or do whatever you need to do to get back to the place where you can listen. Make sure you have fully understood the other person before offering your response.

It is important - particularly when things are difficult to learn - to respond to the other person without shame or blame. Shame and blame only start or prolong a conflict and do not move you any closer to real communication. An example of a comment containing shame or blame might be: "You should not have said that; it shows how selfish you are." Or even, "I can't believe that you said that!" It implies the other person was out of line. The reverse response is helpful. "What do you mean?" or "What makes your feel that way?"

Although there have been tons of literature written about how to speak in a polite and reasonable way - and all of these tools are helpful for raising your awareness - in the end, what matters more than anything else is the intent behind your words. Negative intent equals a negative message regardless of how nice you try and make it sound. Another key to speaking is to keep your communications direct. Try not to lose the other person in an extensive description or analysis. Tell them as directly as possible what you want them to know.

Tool #44: Practice with a Friend

Not sure about your communication skills? Get together with a friend and practice talking about your plans. Let your friend speak. See if you can give your friend the feeling of being heard. Try and give your feedback in a way that is clear and helpful. Then reverse, make sure and get feedback from your friend about your communication. Were you clear and to the point? Did your friend understand what you were saying? Did your friend understand what you were requesting from him or her?

Tool #45: Be Clear when Asking for Help

Because you are starting out with your plan, you will probably be asking for lots of help from others. Remember that many people you will come into contact with are very busy. Assume that the other person does not have an infinite amount of time and make sure you use your communications wisely. Make it easy for that person to give you what you need by being clear about when and how you will communicate with them or by asking them what is best for them.

Notions of Success

It used to be popular to imagine amassing as much money as possible regardless of impact on other people or the environment. Working an 80-hour work week and doing what few others could withstand was considered proof of one's superiority as a human. For many, this attitude died with the 1980s; for some, it is still a part of how they view themselves or what the organization they work for expects of them.

More and more, though, this is not the norm. Many people are choosing to be as devoted to their home life, community, and well-being as they are to making money. Life, for these people, includes choices that are for their own well-being as well as for their wallet.

You are only as successful as you are happy. It is a good idea to make sure your life is in order before you begin your project. This will make your project more likely to be successful - and you more likely to be healthier.

Tool #46: What is Important to You?
Pick from this list the categories that are most important to your life. Underline them.

Family
Partner
Children
Friends
Colleagues
Work
Social Life
Vocation
Life Purpose
My Own Business
Volunteering
Creating a Legacy
Community
Spiritual Growth
Religious Beliefs
Spiritual or Religious Practice
Philanthropy
Physical Well-Being
Sports
Fun
Creativity
Hobbies

List how satisfied you are with each area you have chosen by using a scale of 1-5:

1=0% or unsatisfied.
2=25% or slightly satisfied.
3=50% or moderately satisfied.
4=75% or very satisfied.
5=100% or completely satisfied.

My list of my life priorities and my satisfaction with these life priorities is:

Tool #47: Prioritize

Using the list from Tool #46, ask yourself which three categories are you most moved to make changes in first? What is one action that you can take to make a change in each of these three categories? If you find, after doing this exercise, that you are not very happy with your life, I would suggest stopping here and doing the work you need to do in order to balance your life a bit more before moving forward with you business.

My one action in each of these categories is:

The one I am going to start working on today is:

Imbalance

Even though we may want to rewrite what we consider success to be, the work of many visionaries is just as demanding as a CEO's - even if the motivation is completely different. Some people falsely think that - because they work at home, for themselves, or at what they love - they don't need to make clear boundaries between their work and the rest of their life. This is absolutely not the case. I would be willing to argue that the more you love your work, the more important it is that you set up some clear boundaries so that it does not seep into every part of your life.

I had someone say to me once that part of the root meaning of the word "passion" is "to suffer." Those people who are truly passionate about what they do can probably relate to this definition of passion - to be passionate about something can mean to be consumed and driven by it. So, for the passionate among us, where is balance? Passion might compel you to write at 3am and to work for days without showering, with little sleep, and little food.

Anyone who has been passionately connected to his or her work knows that the self is not always maintained in the process. The creative element - an essential part of envisioning and passionate action - may require dissolution of the self. This makes achieving a deep understanding of balance a challenge.

However, if we substitute "caring for ourselves" for "balance," we get a bit closer to something that might serve those of us who are so intimately connected with our passion. While balance might imply that we spend a certain amount of time doing separate activities, caring for ourselves implies that we are an essential part of our passionate work.

It is important to remember that if we are not healthy, then our work is not healthy. Period - no exceptions. While the metaphysics of this statement are intriguing, some questions will help us more in the end. How might your approach to work change if you looked at it from this fresh perspective? What would you be willing to settle for in terms of self-care?

Tool #48: Self-Care Check-In

What do you do to sustain yourself while you maintain your passionate pursuits?

List five things:

1.
2.
3.
4.
5.

Burn-Out

If you have been working at your project for a while and you have not managed to create a balanced, passionate approach to your project, then, chances are, you are experiencing some burn-out or, if not, then you will be soon. Burn-out looks like this: We started down this road for a reason. We wanted to make a difference. We wanted to do something that was deeply satisfying. Then, at some point, maybe, it just started to seem like a bunch of work. Or maybe, we got so stressed out that, even though we knew it was something we enjoyed, we did not end up enjoying it.

If you have begun to think you might be happier working as a sales clerk at Macy's, then you may have forgotten the reason you started down this path to begin with.

Signs that you have forgotten:
You feel drained rather than energized.
You find that your efforts are not yielding desired results.
You are unable to make quick and accurate decisions.
You are high-strung or stressed out.
You are wondering if you are doing the right thing.

Tool #49: Did You Say Yes?
If you though yes when reading the previous statements, then you will want to apply some of the remedies below.

Get Back on Track
Take a break.
Revisit your mission statement.
Revisit your value statements.
List the top ten reasons you started this business. Pick the top three and see if they are part of your business right now. If they are not, find ways to bring them back in.
Take care of yourself again.

Tool #50: Did You Answer No?
The simple rule: you are an essential part of your business - your health and well-being directly affect your ability to make good decisions and work effectively. If you are not experiencing burn-out, here are some easy, but essential, steps to prevent it.

Make eating healthy food a simple part of your life. Always have some on-hand.
Get adequate sleep and make sure you exercise.
Make time to spend with family and friends.
Schedule breaks - time just to yourself.

Start-Up Basics

Business Bare Minimum Basics

There are some things that will need to be in place for your business/project. So here is a short list of essentials. The Dummies Guide to Business - pick your type - are helpful for an overview of what a business or project takes.

Tool #51: Bare Minimum Checklist

Do you have these things in place?

1. Website/domain name
2. Business card
3. Phone line
4. Business license
5. Liability insurance
6. Billing system/accountant

Marketing Bare Minimum Basics

People need to know what you are doing in order for it to be a success. Really understanding marketing requires that you learn from someone who really understands marketing, but here are a couple of ways to boost the visibility of your business. When you have some capital you will benefit from hiring an expert. The right person will save you lots of money in the end.

Tool #52: Five To-Dos To Get You Started Marketing

1. Create meaningful and personally driven content for your business Website.
2. Use a designer for your Website and business card - professionalism helps.
3. Write an announcement letter and send it to friends, family, and colleagues.
4. Post your business or project on other Internet sites to increase your site visibility.
5. Talk to anyone and everyone you can about what you are planning.

Good marketing is the key to your success. It is advisable to spend money and time developing and getting help developing this part of your project.

One-Page Business Plan

You can synthesize your work and simplify your planning by following a one-page business plan model. When you are not planning on submitting your business plan for funding - or your business is a small more personal venture - this document might be all that you need to stay clear about your business objectives and goals. An example is below. You can also check out http://www.onepagebusinessplan.com/sample_plans.html for more industry-specific samples-

Therapy Unlimited LLC
Business Plan Summary

Vision:
Within two years, Therapy Unlimited will be an established practice grossing $500,000 per year specializing in holistic practices for healing and improving quality of life.

Mission:
Improve people's quality of life through holistic services.

Objectives:
Partner Revenue at $150,000 per partner in two years.
$50,000 for a deposit on a building in one year.

Strategies:
Four therapeutic associates working 60-80 hours per week combined.
Two to four complimentary therapists renting space and practising under the umbrella name Therapy Unlimited..
Create useful tracks and programming.

Plans:
Develop marketing plan.
Establish practitioner partnerships.
Create services profile: individual session, groups, workshops and series.
Hire associates.

Tool #53: Write your own one-page business plan

Mission:

Vision:

Objectives:

Strategies:

Plans:

A Reminder:
Four Words to Remember

In order to sustain your focus, learn what you need to learn, and overcome the obstacles that you might encounter - either inside or outside of yourself - you will need to remember these extremely important four words:

I CAN DO IT.

You can see your dreams and visions become part of this world. As I said in the beginning of this guide, the world is waiting for you to do it. The universe wants you to do it; that is why you have the dream in the first place. Remembering this is what makes your plan have the staying power to become reality.

There are, inevitably, difficult times ahead. No matter how much you know and plan, there will be times when it seems impossible or when you are bearing the burden of having made a major mistake. But, your ability to accept the inevitability of these difficult times, to be willing to walk through them with the belief that "I can do it" that will, in the end, be the true reason why you succeeded. It is the remembering - the getting back up after defeat or failure - that yields the real results.

While this might seem like a twisted pep talk, I know that our willingness to face difficulty and persevere with heart and hope opens us to a richer, more fulfilling life - a life of passion and purpose, a life of doing the work that we were meant to do. I wish this for you. I believe that, if you have heard the call, then you have what you need to make it happen.

Resources

Books and Articles

Heart-Centered Business Strategy by Steven Cady

Rich Dad, Poor Dad by Robert T. Kiyosaki

Getting Things Done by David Allen

Think and Grow Rich by Napoleon Hill

Where Did the Money Go by Ellen Rohr

Driven To Distraction by Edward M. Hallowell

Small Business for Dummies by Eric Tyson and Jim Schell

Book Yourself Solid by Michael Port

Real Answers by Kate Siner

All Marketers are Liars by Seth Godin

Organizations and Programs

Nolo: http://www.nolo.com

SBA: http://www.sba.com

Your local Chamber of Commerce

All Business: http://www.allbusiness.com

Entrepreneur: http://www.entrepreneur.com

Inc: http://www.inc.com/

SCORE: http://www.score.org/index.html

Tools for Business Success: http://www.toolsforbusiness.info/

Additional Tools

Organization:

Planner Pads: https://plannerpads.com

Google Calendar: http://www.google.com/apps/intl/en/business/calendar.html

Domain Names and Website hosting:

GoDaddy: http://www.godaddy.com

1&1: http://www.1and1.com

Tax ID:

IRS: http://www.irs.gov/businesses/small/

MAKE IT HAPPEN!

A **"GET IT DONE"** GUIDE FOR DREAMERS AND VISIONARIES

Kate Siner , Ph.D

www.ingramcontent.com/pod-product-compliance
Lightning Source LLC
Chambersburg PA
CBHW052054190326
41519CB00002BA/215